LONDONERS REM
LIVING THR
THE BL]

C000268663

COMPILED BY THE AGE EXCHANGE REMINISCENCE GROUP

EDITED BY PAM SCHWEITZER

CONTRIBUTORS

Frank Ball	Elsie House
Dorothy Barton	Margaret Kippin
Flo Batley	Doris Lawrence
Lilian Burnett	Elsie Lehane
Ellen Clark	Joyce Milan
Babs Downes	Gwen Parrish
Milly Gardner	Joan Pearce
Bill Herring	Margaret Phair
Joan Herring	Vivien Prince
Doris Hollands	Irene Swanton

This book was launched to coincide with the production of THE BLITZ SHOW by the Age Exchange Youth Theatre and Reminiscence Group, which played as part of the Greenwich Festival 1991.

Age Exchange gratefully acknowledge generous financial support with this project from Thames/LWT Telethon Trust and Age Resource.

Photographs are either from the Imperial War Museum collection, from the contributors themselves, or by Alex Schweitzer.

The front cover photograph shows a photo-collage by members of the Age Exchange Youth Theatre. From this design they produced a painted backcloth for "The Blitz Show", based on the memories in this book.

1

INTRODUCTION

LIVING THROUGH THE BLITZ is a collection of memories compiled by older people at the Age Exchange Reminiscence Centre. Most of the contributors are members of the Reminiscence Group which meets at the Centre to work on recordings and writings about their own lives. We choose themes which are significant to the group and which will have a wide social and historical interest. Members share their recollections and in so doing trigger each other's memories in a series of enjoyable and productive afternoons. Many of the group will then go away and write down what they have recalled, and these written versions are again brought back to the group for comment.

The Blitz project has involved the Reminiscence Group in a wide variety of additional activities. Many have worked closely with the children in the Age Exchange Youth Theatre who have been creating their own show out of these memories of the Blitz. The older people have attended the children's Saturday morning sessions to work with them on improvisations based on their own memories, and to help the children understand what it was like to live through

Members of the Age Exchange Reminiscence Group preparing "Living Through The Blitz". Left to right Dorothy Barton, Pam Schweitzer, Vivien Prince, Joyce Milan, Margaret Phair, Ellen Clark, Edie McHardy and Flo Batley.

Children from the Age Exchange Youth Theatre in an open rehearsal of their show based on these memories of the Blitz.

that period. A considerable degree of mutual respect and appreciation has resulted from these cross-generational sessions, as well as a lot of fun.

The older people have also been involved in the creation of their own play, which they have devised through improvisation. Stories have been told, elaborated, improvised and scripted by the group, who have then gone on to rehearse and learn the scripted scenes. At the launch of this book, the pensioners read some of their own stories and enacted others. The children presented their versions of the scenes they had worked on with the pensioners, with each storyteller introducing her own scene.

It is for this sort of creative use of reminiscence that Age Exchange is best known. We believe that working together creatively across the generations, both on the recollection and the interpretation of the past, is the most effective way of making memories matter.

PAM SCHWEITZER

3

7th SEPTEMBER 1940

I have a vivid memory of most of the events of this day, and can still picture the scenes.

It was a beautiful late summer day, with scarcely a cloud in a blue sky. We were living at the time in Fossil Road, Lewisham, about five minutes walk away from Hilly Fields.

In the afternoon I decided to take a walk over the Hill. I can remember my mood, I felt a sense of well-being, felt "good". I can even recall what I was wearing at the time, a favourite dress which somehow went with this mood.

As I walked across the grass, I saw a friend of mine sitting on the slope. He was one of the balloon barrage boys and we had been friends since the previous January. I sank down on the grass beside him, and we sat chatting in a desultory fashion, not discussing the war. It should be made clear that we weren't obsessed with the war, we didn't "eat, sleep and drink it". It was as though our lives consisted of two separate compartments, running in parallel lines, which from time to time would converge. We were not unaware of what was happening, and I had worries concerning my elder brother who was on active service with the Navy, but we had to get on with our lives.

I remember looking out across the park, and, apart from the balloon barrage site, it was almost like a peace-time Saturday afternoon, children playing happily, the lush green grass, trees still in full foliage, a very pleasant scene.

We decided to wander up to the cafe for a cup of tea, and I can recall bemoaning the fact that my Saturdays in future wouldn't be so free. I was working for the Electric Light Company, and because so much time had been wasted due to long periods in the air-raid shelter as a result of the "nuisance" or "hit and run" raids to which we had been subjected for the past few weeks, it was decided that a skeleton staff would have to operate on Saturdays, and I was to be on the first shift.

Whilst we were drinking our tea, the Air Raid warning sounded, but we didn't take a lot of notice, assuming it was another "nuisance" raid. We finished our tea and as we came out of the cafe and looked down the hill, there was quite a transformation – the place was practically empty, just a few mothers with their children scuttling towards the entrance. As we looked up at the sky we noticed puffs of smoke and began to hear the thud of bombs and noise of ack-ack fire (there was a large anti-aircraft gun on the other side of the hill). We looked at each other, and he said, "This is something more than a nuisance raid, you'd better come into our shelter". So we ran down the slope to the large Anderson type shelter on the site. A few mothers and children, who had further to go to get home, were already there, and we tried to keep the children amused. I can't remember whether the all-clear eventually went, or whether there was a lull. I think it was the former and the boys advised us to get home quickly.

When I arrived home, my mother was waiting at the gate. My brothers and I had all been out, so she was anxiously awaiting our safe return. The local air raid warden came over and told me that the Electric Light Company had been bombed. I felt awful, bearing in mind my former facetious remark, that "If they bomb my firm, I won't have to go to work". My eighteen year old brother had booked seats at the Lewisham Hippodrome for the evening performance, and said he would still go. My mother begged him not to, and when I expressed my intention of going down to see what the situation was at my firm, she used this, asking him to go with me to, "look after your sister". Poor lad had to agree.

I arrived at the building, to find there were already many members of staff and management on the spot. Mercifully the only casualty had been the caretaker's dog (what a different story it would have been if this was a week later!) It appears that the building had been hit by an aerial torpedo which exploded when reaching the girders of the first floor, destroying the offices, whilst the showroom on the ground floor had less damage. Our ledgers were kept on the large cards and these were scattered all over the place. We all helped to collect as many as we could. The smell of cordite and singed papers was something we would get used to. We were told that we would be informed what was to happen the following week and that there would be a member of the staff in the air raid shelter (which wasn't damaged) to give out information for those of us living near enough.

That night the heavy raids continued. At that time we didn't have an Anderson, but my father had made our dining room as bomb proof as possible by lashing our large mahogany dining table in front of the french windows and moving all the beds downstairs. I remember that night very clearly, the noise of the bombs and ack-ack guns (so near to us). What I hated worst was the screaming bombs. My fifteen-year-old-brother was a messenger with the A.F.S. and when he didn't arrive home in the early hours of the morning, following the all-clear, we were all worried. We went out locally, walking the streets, but couldn't find him, so my father went down to the A.F.S. station, and was told that he had in fact left after the all-clear. My father decided to have a look round the building, and found him fast asleep on a heap of coke! They told my father he had worked very hard, and was obviously so exhausted he just couldn't manage to walk home.

MARGARET KIPPIN

ABSOLUTE TERROR

It all started innocently enough, on a beautiful Saturday afternoon. My cousin and I were playing in my grandmother's garden. I had been evacuated away almost exactly one year, and as my foster home was only an hour or so away, I often came home for a short spell during school holidays. I was due to go back to Cranbrook in Kent in a week's time.

It was the constant drone of planes that first caught our attention. When we looked up we saw mile upon mile of black dots in the sky and then the siren went.

We all ran to the Anderson shelter in absolute terror. This was the first time it had ever been used. No carpets or chairs had been put in, there had been no need up until then. I know my cousin and I instinctively crouched down on the dry dirt, our hands over our ears. Then we heard the first bomb, a whistle and a crunch which sounded right outside the door, though in fact it was over the water. Silvertown, Tate and Lyle buildings and all along the river were being bombed. Our side of the river was to catch it later.

There was a lull. When dusk came the sky was already red from all the burning buildings, and was a good guide for the next wave of bombers.

When the siren went again I was in my own home just over the road from my grandmother's, but our shelter had not been finished. The Siemens factory was at the bottom of our garden and could have been a prime target, so we all ran to my grandmother's shelter again, and amazingly, what I remember most in all that horror was a very painful splinter I got down my fingernail from the back garden gate!

Our own house was made unsafe from that first series of raids. I never saw my house or my grandmother's house again after that night raid, and most of my things went missing.

We were all in a state of shock. Needless to say I was sent back to Cranbrook immediately with some members of my family. We all stayed with my foster family who managed to put them up somewhere, anywhere just until things were sorted out back in London.

I went back to Cranbrook recently and I will never work out how at least nine people stayed in that house. My foster mum was a genius.

JOAN PEARCE

A Heinkel III aircraft over the Thames, as seen from another German aircraft.

TRAVELLING UNDER FIRE

I cast my mind back fifty years. It isn't hard to do, in fact in a lot of ways it is as if it were yesterday.

It was even before I was married. The year before, in 1939, I had started my new job, just before the war, in a well-known firm of retail chemists. I was in their main London office and I qualified for a few days holiday the very week the war started, which to say the least was eventful.

In 1940, I picked my own holiday week and eagerly looked forward to the 7th September. It was the weekend that Hitler decided to unleashed his horror on London, the Blitz.

That day, with my mother and sister, we went to see my grandmother who lived at Blackheath. We were on our way home that afternoon when all hell was let loose. We caught a bus to Lewisham, then a tram on to the Downham Estate where we lived. The drone of aeroplanes, the sound of ack-ack, the "woof" of the big guns and the shrapnel falling, were all very frightening.

They became even more so when our tram would not go any farther than Southend Village. To go on home, half way up Downham Way, it was walk or run as much as possible. The three of us decided to chance it, more running than walking, with shrapnel falling around us. We didn't even think how dangerous it would be. We just wanted to get home to my dad, who was indoors and probably out of his mind with worry. We made it, all three of us in one piece (each)!

This was the forerunner of what followed day after day. At first it was just day raids. My dear mum used to meet me at Grove Park Station to make sure I was all right, never worrying about her own safety.

We had what was called an Anderson air-raid shelter in the garden. As I came in one night to the sirens proclaiming another air-raid, my mother grabbed my dinner out of the gas oven with a tea towel and thrust it into my hands en route to the garden shelter. It was red-hot in my hands. She went down the steps to the shelter, first steadying my arm with my red hot dinner. I got to the bottom of the three steps with the minced meat, potatoes and carrots (still remembered after all this time) and the meal turned turtle all over the ground, leaving one very hungry daughter until much later.

At first we lost a great deal of time at work when the sirens went and we had to trot down to the shelter (the store house for their supplies in the basement). How cold it was down there, I remember. The cost in man-hours to the business must have been tremendous, and soon a fire-watching rota was introduced for spotting incendiary bombs and the German planes that dropped them. This was all done voluntarily, and it went on for twenty-four hours a day in one-hour stints, but no ladies or girls were allowed on the roof after half-past five, when trading stopped for the night. It was only when the fire-watchers decided that the raiders in the skies were in the immediate vicinity that we had internal bells and then we had to make our way in an orderly fashion to an allocated spot in the shelter.

Incidentally a civilian fire-watch was started in our road from six at night to six in the morning, in one hour stints rotating one hour each week. You hammered on the door of your relief and handed him or her your tin hat before you were allowed to go home yourself. Many's the time in the small hours I would not get up out of bed and my mum did it for me.

It was a nasty experience if one happened to be in a train when there was a raid. I can remember one such occasion going to work. The train got stopped on the railway bridge going over the river, not a very healthy spot to be in an air-raid. You could get taken into any London terminus through raid damage to the rail system. We were there for hours in the middle of a heavy air-raid. After a while those that had seats in the train exchanged places with those standing to give them a rest. People got hungry and lunch packets came out and were offered all round the fellow-passengers. There was a great camaraderie amongst people. I got to work at five o'clock, ready to go home at half past five!

At work we never knew which way we would be going home. There might be a direct hit on one of the London Stations. Somehow the firm found out and would inform us about half hour before finishing time. I never asked how they got this information. I never even thought about it.

I must mention one hilarious (or so it seemed to me) form of transport. All the London stations were closed one night, through landmines, bomb damage, fires etc. It was every man (or woman) for himself. While I was waiting for a bus or tram, a hearse drew up and the driver said he was going to Dulwich Village. Three of us climbed aboard. It was near enough and we could worry about the rest of the journey when we got there. It was quite safe to do that kind of thing then, the only danger being from the enemy. I can't remember how I made my way home from Dulwich Village to Downham that night.

DORIS LAWRENCE

A helpful motorist with a destination notice behind his windscreen.
He is being hailed by a prospective passenger.

HITLER'S DAYS ARE NUMBERED

After the fall of France in June 1940, invasion of Britain by the Germans seemed inevitable, but with blind faith inspired by the speeches of Winston Churchill, everybody went about their business with grim determination that no enemy would set foot in our country. (It would have been a case of up brooms and at 'em!)

Our heroes were the fighter pilots who we knew were facing overwhelming odds, and it was awful to hear of the losses they suffered. Planes were also being destroyed on the ground when airfields were bombed, but it was the pilots who couldn't be replaced and to whom we owed so much.

I believe it was in August that the first bomb dropped in Charlton Lane destroying St. Paul's Church. Our family then lived in 107 Elliscombe Road, which was very close by as a plane flies, so I felt the little heroine. Another incident in August earned me a ticking off by my father as I sat in the cinema in Beresford Square during a raid and a plane crashed nearby. Those raids were a nuisance but did not cause much fear.

The 7th September changed all that and we all learned the hard way what fear was. That day started off happily for our family as we were moving across the road to live in a house, after spending the three years since we came from Aberdeen in upstairs flats with no direct access to the garden.

Anyhow, my mother, father and myself were clearing up in the old flat when the siren sounded in the afternoon. Thinking it was to be a hit-and-run affair, as before, we didn't go to the Anderson shelter. My older brother, an apprentice engineer, was working and the younger one on duty as an air raid wardens' messenger. The family downstairs, whose kitchen we had to go through to the garden, were out.

Very soon we were aware of the sound of heavy bombers and lots of noise, a combination of exploding bombs and gunfire. Realising this was what we were expecting and dreading, we were down in that shelter in record time just as we were – all our belongings were in the house across the road. It's the terrible noise I can remember and the shaking of the shelter. At that time I could not differentiate between the sound of bombs and gunfire.

When the all-clear sounded and we emerged, a terrible sight awaited us as the smoke from the burning docks was billowing everywhere in thick black clouds. The two girls who lived next door and I walked along Charlton Road to the Village and we met many people who'd been caught out shopping, etc., and were trudging home – all with the same shocked look. It was an awesome sight looking down upon the river and across to North Woolwich and the Isle of Dogs – just flames and smoke. It seemed that nobody or nothing could have survived such fire – a ship could also be seen burning.

Of course the bombers returned later and those fires were a target for the high explosive bombs. The fear then was that this was a forerunner of invasion. Luckily this was not so – we were spared that, but suffered many more days and nights of raids.

Anyhow, in our new home we settled not in the bedrooms but in the cellar, which was more comfortable (if that is an apt word) for sheltering in comparative safety than in the Anderson shelter in the old home which we would have had to share with the family in the lower flat. It proved to be a fortunate move as, although we never had the full use of the house (which was extremely badly damaged the following May, making it uninhabitable) the one we left was much worse as a land mine fell next to it.

In spite of the raids it was necessary to get to work each day and those journeys were adventures of sorts. When main roads were impassable one got to know back turnings and got used to travelling on all sorts of vehicles – there was always an assortment of folks on the backs of lorries. Motor cycles were the best as they could get through more easily. Of course walking was often the only way and we all tried not to be late for work however we got there.

Everybody got adept at hitting the deck quickly if the whistle of an unexpected bomb was heard. Any housewife worth her salt woud not lose her place if she was queuing for sausages, fish or other unrationed food. Their stamina and sense of humour were terrific and there were some enlightening discussions about how best to dispose of Hitler if they got their hands on him. There was a wonderful companionship all round which helped each and every one of us over the bad patches when homes were lost and those close to us became casualties. Like everything good or bad, raids and overhead dog-fights became a way of life which we had to endure and life certainly was far from being all doom and gloom.

My father was a staff refrigerating engineer with the Blue Star Line, so his life became a continuous move to docks all over the country. It was never known until the last minute into which dock the convoys bringing essential food would come, as that would be an invitation to the bombers. His was, I feel, quite a hazardous job, as was all work involved in getting supplies to us.

I worked at West Park, Eltham, where the Gas Company had taken over numbers 39 and 41 for offices – they had houses dotted all over the area for this purpose as did other large firms. The Gas Works in Old Kent Road, where the Head Office used to be, was, of course, a prime target.

Edie in the W.A.A.F. 1941.

When the war started it was guaranteed that all staff in the Armed Forces would have their wages made up to what they would earn if working. However, so many were going into the Forces that they had to stop doing this for those who volunteered as it was costing too much, I suppose. There were also rumours that the gas industry would become a reserved occupation.

For a long time I'd been keen to go into the Air Force and there was a great recruiting drive for women volunteers to release men from certain trades to be trained for air crew. Conscription for women would eventually come, so my future was very uncertain. At the end of 1940 there was a concentrated raid on the City and much damage was caused by fire and high explosives. That seemed to motivate me, and I called at the Yorkshire Grey recruiting office and got enrolment papers.

On February 24th 1941 the course of the war took a new turn. I joined the Air Force. Hitler's days were numbered!!!! Admittedly it did take four-and-a-half years.

EDIE McHARDY

BIKING THROUGH THE BLITZ

September 1940 found me working in Woolwich Arsenal, where I had been since the outbreak of war.

I must go back to Day One of the war to give an idea of the labour content of the arms factory. The Arsenal was flooded with applicants for work, many thrown out of a job because their type of employment was not considered essential to the war effort, but also many who had given up their jobs to enter the Arsenal in the hope of being reserved during the span of hostilities.

Thus the factory was teeming with inexperienced labour with little to do and plenty of time to do it in. From the outbreak of hostilities to the first air-raid, scores of A.R.P. wardens who were employed by the Arsenal spent many remunerative hours, days and weeks playing cards, or getting in as much sleep as possible so they could do "private work" during the few off-duty hours their job provided.

To me, after spending a life-time of "nose to the grindstone" in the building industry, this state of affairs was a novelty, but by September 1940 I was feeling very ashamed of how little I was contributing to the war effort, which consequently encouraged me to seek release from the factory for more worthwhile employment elsewhere.

When I arrived at the Arsenal for work the morning after the first air-raid to affect the S.E. area of London, I was met with utter chaos. Many of the Arsenal A.R.P. squad had deserted their posts, and their expertise, so badly needed, was unavailable. The "inexperienced" labour force (building maintenance workers) of which I was one, was suddenly considered experienced enough to handle the emergency, and it made me feel proud of my colleagues to see the way they tackled the gruesome tasks of unearthing bodies, putting out fires, and all the other horrors that are the aftermath of enemy attack from the air.

Things were not any better for me at home. My parents had a nice detatched bungalow at Albany Park, which suffered damage from a bomb that fell too close for comfort. It was my parents' bedroom and the lounge that were most badly affected, and my parents, who were in bed at the time, were injured – not too badly, fortunately, but enough to be taken to hospital. My precious collection of almost ten thousand 78 rpm records, which were stored in the lounge, became my precious EX-collection.

While my parents were in hospital and I spent a few days with my sister, the bungalow became a prey to looters, who stripped it bare, not only of damaged goods but anything they could lay their hands on. They even disconnected

A notice warning all that the penalty for looting may be death.

and stole the kitchen sink! Pilfering was one of the most odious outcomes of the bombing, and people caught doing it by neighbours of those being pilfered were made to feel it was not a good idea.

My nephew, who was in the Territorial Army at the outbreak of war, was immediately called up and sent to an army camp at Hooe, in Kent. He was buying a motorcycle from dealers at Brixton, name of Pride and Clarke, on hire purchase. Because of being called up, the bike became a liability, and he decided to return it to the dealers. Having paid nine of the twelve instalments I thought this a disastrous move on his part, and said I would take over the bike and complete the transaction.

This is how I came to be riding a motor-cycle to friends at Abbey Wood during the afternoon of an air-raid. My journey was via Danson Road, into Brampton Road, and down Knee Hill into Abbey Wood. Despite the fact that an air-raid was in progress, my journey was uneventful till I got to Bostall Heath. On the Heath an ack-ack division was sited, complete with six-inch naval guns. Just as I was passing they opened up, and the noise was so deafening, coupled with the blast, that I was thrown off the bike. Fortunately, neither the bike nor myself were too badly affected, and I continued my journey to Abbey Wood. I stayed with my friends a bit longer than was wise, and started my homeward journey in pitch-black. The bike's lighting, as regulations demanded, was reduced to a glimmer, and I found myself wandering all over the road.

I finally reached Danson Road, but while I was at Abbey Wood a bomb had dropped in Danson Road, leaving a large crater, into which the bike and I tumbled. The bike suffered a buckled front wheel and a punctured petrol tank, but I escaped with a few minor scratches.

During the time of the Blitz, I was courting a girl, later to become my wife, who lived with her parents in a council house in Downham Way. It was my practice to visit there every Saturday and stay overnight. They had an Anderson shelter in the garden, which, because of the restricted size of the garden, was rather close to the house. When the air-raid warning sounded the four of us, my wife-to-be, her parents and myself, would make for the shelter. We were in the shelter the evening a bomb made a direct hit on four houses, including that of my wife's parents. We were trapped in the shelter, which was covered in dirt and brick rubble, for almost four hours before being dug out. The experience of being buried alive was traumatic and the wife's mother had a mild stroke which left her face permanently disfigured.

Another experience I had with the motor-cycle was on the morning after London's first big raid. A friend of mine, who was in the Auxiliary Fire Service and stationed at the Fire Brigade's headquarters on the Embankment, was desperate to get to work, but all public service vehicles were at a standstill, so I offered to take her on the bike. The ride was hectic all the way, to say the least. At times were were wading through brick rubble, bumping over hose pipes, and continually being diverted where progress, even for a bike, was impossible. We eventually made the journey, and once there my friend had a make-shift bed in the station till the roads became reasonably usable again.

My brother was in the City of London Police, and during the Blitz he and his colleagues had a rough passage. Most of them vowed they would gladly change places with service men in any of the Armed Forces.

FRANK BALL

ST. PAUL'S SURVIVES

On September 7th 1940 at about five o'clock, hundreds of German bombers followed the Thames through London, dropping high explosive and incendiary bombs as they went, so that both banks of the river were alight. Later that evening they came back and by the light of the fires, destroyed most of the Docks and a lot of the East End.

I remember these two raids so well because I was alone at the time in our house in an outer suburb of London. My parents, with my younger brother and sister, had gone to visit relations at Peckham and Deptford, but I hadn't felt like going with them. They had expected to be back by tea-time, so when they weren't and the raid started, I assumed they'd taken shelter and would get back as soon as possible after the "All clear". When the second raid began without any sign of them, I was really worried and frightened, but I didn't go into our Anderson shelter in the back garden in case news of them got through to me, so I made up a bed under the dining table, and lay there with my dog Pat. I hardly slept all night, not only because of the noise of the bombers droning overhead, but also I was worried about my family.

Our district didn't seem to be the target that night, but I realized that my family might be in considerable danger. I was glad I'd stayed in the house, however, because in the middle of the night someone came to tell me that they were stuck in Deptford and couldn't get home! Dad had managed to relay a message to me through a number of different people, mainly friends and relations, because we were not on the telephone and neither were any of our neighbours. The message took six or seven hours to reach me, but at least it got there eventually.

When they arrived home on Sunday morning, they told me how some of the Docks were still burning when they left and how, according to Dad, "The river had been alight from Woolwich upwards." Apparently he'd gone down to have a look very early in the morning because he'd worked in the Docks for a good part of his life.

That was the first of fifty-seven consecutive nights of bombing on London. Then there was a short lull, then night raids continued until early in 1941, with two particularly bad raids on December 8th and 29th.

I was working not far from Fenchurch Street at this time as a book-keeper/typist, and travelled to work by train to London Bridge, then walked from there. The trains, all with single closed carriages and "Ladies only" compartments in those days, had blackout curtains at the windows. The ordinary light bulbs were removed and replaced with blue tinted very dim

During an air-raid on London the freakish effect of the blast of one bomb held a bus, empty of passengers, against one side of an adjoining house so that its radiator rested almost on the 2nd floor window, 8th September, 1940.

bulbs, making it almost impossible to see the person sitting opposite. However, the trains usually ran on time and even when the big London terminals were hit during a raid as they sometimes were, trains were disorganised for only a short while.

It was a bit nerve-wracking travelling home in winter, not being able to see inside or outside the train, and wondering how safe we would be if the train was bombed. Fortunately I never had to find out.

The Blitz continued night after night, with not much enemy activity during the day, and every evening we'd settle down in our Anderson shelter which Dad had made very comfortable with four bunk beds, a rag rug on the floor, and a hurricane lamp hanging from a hook. There was also an Aladdin paraffin heater for when the weather was cold. My father was a part-time Air Raid Warden, and usually went on duty when the siren sounded, or as soon as possible after he'd come home from his job in the Docks.

I'd lie in my bunk with my dog Pat on my feet, if I wasn't on firewatching duty, listening to the bombers overhead, and the roar of anti-aircraft guns, and would eventually fall asleep despite the noise, which seems amazing now when I look back to that time.

Not long before Christmas 1940, I was on firewatching duty during a raid which had started about tea-time, accompanied by my father because my usual partner was late. It soon became obvious that it was going to be a bad night, so Dad told me to go home to be with the rest of the family, and he walked with me to the corner of our road before going on to the A.R.P. Wardens' post to report for duty. As I turned towards our house a few yards away I heard Dad talking to someone I couldn't see, then I pushed open our front door and went inside. I'd hardly got into the passage when there was a tremendous explosion and our house rocked sideways, while windows, ceiling and doors flew about. I managed to throw myself into the living room, where I was dragged under the table by my mother, who was sheltering there with the younger children.

A few minutes later there was another explosion and the house rocked the other way, accompanied by the crash of still more falling debris, both inside and out, soon afterwards Dad ran in, grabbed the cloth off the table and dashed out again without giving any explanation and apparently without noticing the damage to the house.

We crouched under the table not knowing what to do until police and wardens came to help us out and escort us across to the Anderson shelter, already crowded with neighbours, including several small children. We sat on upright dining chairs so close together that our feet almost touched in the circle we made, about a dozen adults, not counting children, with only a small nightlight to give a glimmer of light. I sat there all night with my dog on my lap, listening to the noise from outside and wondering what was happening out there, occasionally dozing off with my head resting on the dog.

In the morning we came out of the shelter to find that two landmines had fallen in our short road, causing a great deal of damage. Our home could be used, although we couldn't get upstairs, and doors, windows and some ceilings were missing, as well as some furniture and possessions damaged.

One mine had fallen in a small wooded area so the blast had been slightly diverted, but the other had landed directly on the home of a young couple with three little boys. They had been on their way home after doing some shopping and were the people I had heard speak to my father the night before. The mine went off as they walked up their garden path and the whole family were killed except for the six-month old baby, who was found alive in his dead mother's arms. The tablecloth my father took out of our house was used to cover the remains of the two little boys after Dad had collected them together, as they'd been blown to pieces.

Although several other neighbours were killed at the same time, it was the death of this little family that affected us all so much, especially Dad, who had

A bombed out family is shown hospitality by neighbours – the ruins of their house can be seen across the road.

bad dreams for weeks afterwards. My father was very lucky indeed that night because he was only a few yards away when the mine exploded, but he was only badly bruised and shocked as he was hurled across the road, although a young woman who had just walked past him was killed.

Most of the men in our road decided not to go to work that morning after the raid, but stayed at home to help each other clear up the mess and do what repairs they could.

My parents thought I would be better off at work, so after a quick wash in the kitchen I set off for my City office in the clothes I had sat up in all night! I must say I was relieved to find that the girl I worked with also looked fairly scruffy, because she'd been bombed out too, and had spent the night in the Underground, also sleeping in her clothes.

Our boss sent us home at lunchtime, and that night we went into our own

Anderson shelter as soon as the siren sounded. Dad was still badly shocked, so Mum and I persuaded him to stay in the shelter with us for once.

On December 29th there was another huge raid on London, mainly in the City, and as I travelled to work the next morning, I could see fires burning all over the place, and realized that there must have been a great deal of damage, but it was worse than anything I could have imagined.

As I turned on to London Bridge from the station I looked to the left and could see St. Paul's Cathedral standing alone in an area of complete devastation. The air was full of smoke and the smell of burning, with dust from the debris over everything. As I looked at Wren's masterpiece I felt a lump in my throat because, like so many people I felt that while St. Pauls survived, so would we.

Halfway across the bridge a group of exhausted firemen, with smoke-blackened faces and clothes, were rolling up their hoses after battling with fires all night. Quite spontaneously, the office workers broke into a cheer and several shook hands with firemen as they passed. I was in tears as I walked along, it was such an emotional moment. I don't think anyone should ever forget that firemen were heroes during the entire war, especially during the Blitz.

When I reached my office building I found it was the only one still standing, comparatively undamaged in a street blocked with rubble. My boss was there with some of the other staff, so after scrambling over the debris, we all started trying to clear up inside the building, sweeping out glass, and looking for ledgers and other documents.

Suddenly a policeman rushed in and said "Everybody out, there's an unexploded bomb in the backyard". Pausing only to grab my handbag and the ledgers I was responsible for, I made my way to the end of the street again, where all the staff gathered with various bits of office equipment in their arms. After a while, someone from another firm nearby offered us space in their building, so we all made our way there.

It was a bitterly cold day, with a smattering of snow on the ground, and there was no gas, water or electricity in the City, which meant no heating on and no cups of tea. We worked in our temporary office with all our outdoor clothes on, and it was obvious that unless we found hot food and drink fairly soon, we should all have to return home, so Jean (our other typist) and I took an early lunchbreak and went out to see what we could find. We had both worked in the area for some time and thought we knew our way about, but after a few minutes of detouring round blocked off streets we were completely lost, without familiar buildings to guide us.

Suddenly we fancied we could smell something cooking, so walking along sniffing like a couple of Bisto kids, we followed the tantalising smell until it led us to a small restaurant, minus all doors and windows, where the enterprising owner was cooking sausages and mash over bottled gas stoves. We joined the all male queue and counted lovely brown sizzling sausages to see if there were enough for us, and when we arrived at the counter we were handed a plate of two sausages, a pile of mashed potatoes, and a huge mug of hot strong tea for a very small amount of money.

We were looking around for seats when a voice said from behind the counter, "Upstairs please, ladies, it's quite safe, we've checked it", and then I noticed a sign on the wall in gold letters which read "Ladies' dining room" with an elegant hand, ending in a ruff, pointing to the stairs. Jean and I took our food upstairs and ate it in solitary splendour, looking out of non-existent windows over an almost non-existent City, and giggled at the absurdity of not being allowed to eat with the men.

When we got back to our temporary office we told the others what we had found, and they all departed at a run to get their share of sausages and mash. We all packed up and went home about two o'clock so as to be home before dark and the onslaught of another wave of bombers. Surprisingly, within a day or so, all the pipes and broken cables were repaired, our unexploded bomb was removed and we returned to our own building, where the clearing away of debris was carried out around us.

DOROTHY BARTON

MARRIED BLISS BLITZED!

I had been married for eleven months enjoying as a twenty-year-old housewife our new home. Air raids were a disruptive nuisance to be coped with when at home by angrily dashing across a field of allotments to the public shelter. We were even more irate when, returning home one morning, we discovered a break-in. Our front door had been blown open with blast from a 1,000 lb bomb dropped at the bottom of the road, and someone had entered the hall and rifled the electricity meter. Most meters were coin operated in those days and of course they were not being emptied regularly now as there were staff shortages with so many men away on active service.

On another occasion, the blast from a nearby land mine broke the windows and sucked the precious china ornaments (wedding gifts) across the room, scratching our much loved sideboard. This may seem trivial, and, since we were safe, what did it matter? We should have been – and indeed we were – so thankful, but nevertheless at the time I remember being really angry with Adolf Hitler.

I suppose at that stage of the war ignorance was bliss. I and maybe many others did not realise the line was so narrow between victory and defeat. Our saviours were the young Air Force pilots who kept going under very difficult conditions, battling against the mighty Luftwaffe, intent on wiping us out prior to the invasion. As Churchill said, "Never was so much owed by so many to so few".

Our morale was always uplifted by Churchill's speeches. He was so fiercely determined we would win the war, and we did with blood, sweat and tears. This unity of purpose between the civilian population and the forces was even more necessary when, on Saturday 7th September, a beautiful sunny day with bright blue skies, London was reduced to a blackened, smoking pyre.

My husband and I were in our flat at Bexleyheath on the first floor as the siren went. Thinking it was only another short raid, we stayed in the narrow hallway but soon learnt by the noise and drone of hundreds of bombers it was to be something quite different.

This was the beginning of the Blitz and we were to experience more terrible raids to come although at the time we could only be appalled at all the dreadful damage done that afternoon, with more to follow that night as, lit by the many fires started earlier, the enemy came back and wreaked more havoc. Our fire-fighters, Ambulance Service, Air Raid Wardens, with the public included, deserve a medal of the highest category. Everyone did their bit.

We carried on – my husband at his job in the Woolwich Arsenal, a clearing up job now, since his workshop had been flattened. I went to the City by train via strange stations and routes unknown to me, but necessary, due to damage by overnight raids. We got there in the end, often an hour or so late, but we made it.

Exactly one year after our marriage on October 1st 1940 my husband was called into the Royal Air Force and reported to Blackpool, but life went on. I now shared an Anderson shelter with my next door neighbour who was a War Reserve Policeman. These men did their own jobs by day and a series of shifts at night whenever the raids were on. His wife was a very nervous girl, but we enjoyed a laugh one evening when, during a particularly noisy raid, there was a silence, and she said, "Shush, I hear footprints!" It was only her husband checking to see if we were alright, and he joined in the fun of her remark.

My husband made it home for Christmas, due to the efforts of another member of his group who collected a pound from each man and hired a coach to get to London (a week's rent for us in those days). I had managed to get hold of a chicken for dinner, fresh, not frozen of course, and at that time it came complete with head, neck and feet. Never having drawn, cleaned or cooked a chicken previously, we both stood mesmerised with Mrs Beeton's Cookery book (another wedding gift, obviously necessary) open at the ready. The door bell rang. It was the milkman and yes, it was Christmas Day! What a blessing! We asked, had he cleaned a bird before? Being a family man, he had, and so, rewarded with an extra Christmas Box, he did the job for us. Our dinner was secure until the Air Raid Siren went, which of course it did. It was only a nuisance raid this time though, and so we continued eating.

Life went on between raids, which thankfully lessened during the days, but nights were always dreaded and most of them were spent below ground in the Anderson shelter. One raid in particular took the roof off the flat and, being on my own, my husband thought that I should move in with my sister and her husband. That was another pin to stick into Hitler, losing my very first home, but how fortunate we are to be able to write these memories down today. So many thousands of the population weren't so lucky.

IRENE SWANTON

WITH FRIENDS LIKE THAT ...

It was ironic that, having been evacuated a year before September 1940 to avoid the expected destruction of London by bombs, we were mostly back in London when it finally happened. I was ten years old and lived in Yalding Road, Bermondsey.

On "that" Saturday afternoon I had been sent to the baker's around the corner to buy a cut loaf of bread. In those days you bought the loaf, a "square tin" in this case, and it was cut up on a machine like a bacon slicer and put into a paper bag. As I left the shop, the siren started. I leapt on my little bike and hurtled around the corner where my mother and aunt were on the pavement screaming at me to hurry. I jumped off the bike without stopping it and we all raced down to the Anderson shelter. We were near Surrey Docks, the timber docks, and the afternoon was a horrible experience. At the end everyone went out to their front doors, as we always did in those days, but our attention was taken by the sight in the road. My bike still lay on the pavement but the road was strewn with the square and empty crusts of the loaf of bread. Raid or no raid, the sparrows had had a feast!

We soon got used to spending nights (and sometimes hours in the day too) in the shelter. Our shelter was a bit special. My father was a steel erector and he had built a thick re-inforced concrete wall about three feet high and deep into the ground along the side and a brick porch with a reinforced concrete roof over the doorway so that we could descend into the shelter slowly and safely. Inside we had a polished parquet floor! It was well stocked with beds, first-aid equipment, blankets, books, candles and everything we needed. To this day, the smell of mustiness and candles together gives me an immediate flashback.

We had lots of flowers on the top of the shelter and my friends and I used the wall for jumping and playing on. The girl next door jumped off one day and caught herself by the neck on the clothes line. She had a terrible weal but could have broken her neck.

My auntie who lived with us did not like being in the shelter and used to prefer to go "round the arches". The railway arches which ran right across South London provided enormous shelters. One really bad night she panicked and insisted she was going during a raid, demanding that my father took her, but the road was full of hoses and even the road, made of wood blocks and tar, was on fire, so she had to stay put. She left to join her son in Slough the following day.

Londoners got very fed up because there seemed to be no opposition to the night-time raids. I remember the night when there was a terrific noise of guns

going off and it turned out that guns had been put into neighbouring wagons and into parks and fired as much for a morale booster as for effectiveness. I know we all cheered along our line of shelters.

My memory is of light all the time – a yellow light, clear as daylight, every night from the fires. And noise, and shouting and dawn. The raids died away each night and we always seemed to re-emerge in dawn-light. I was always put back to bed but my dad started his daily trek to the aerodrome he was building at Leavesdon near Watford. He was supposed to be in a reserved occupation and not fire-watching at night, but he was in and out all night like everyone else and got very tired. One day he came home and said that he had dropped off to sleep while working on a girder forty feet up and if his mates hadn't shouted at him, he would have fallen. He said we would either have to shelter in an Underground station or go away with him to where he was working. The Underground frightened my mother so we went off to Abbots Langley near Watford. Mum put her bits and pieces of china and glass in a tin boiler and tied the lid on and put it behind a chair in the front room. We took the dog and what we could carry and left.

Before we went, the family next door asked if they could use our shelter as it was better. That very night, the house and, I think, four more of the terrace were bombed. Earlier that week, a mysterious hole had appeared in next door's garden. It was only about four inches wide but no matter how long a pole was put down it, it seemed bottomless. The air raid wardens tried to drop stones down it and probed it with rods and eventually it was left as a puzzle. I suppose it could have been an unexploded bomb but more likely shrapnel. Anyway, either it or another bomb brought down the backs of the houses. The front wall, on the street, remained standing. The family in our shelter were dug out safely, their own shelter demolished.

We were traced through my dad's firm on the Monday. I remember I was sent off to buy some cigarettes while my dad broke the news to my mum. On the Tuesday we travelled back.

The front door was on the top of what remained of the stairs but the lace curtains were still beautifully draped across the passage. There was a neat round tunnel into the mass of rubble to the green, metal kitchen cabinet which was actually holding up the ruins. The cabinet was bare. All the jam, sugar, tins that had been stocked up were gone – looted at great danger to the looter. My father went through too and managed to open the door of the kitchen range where the insurance policies and other certificates had been forgotten when we left. They were still there.

We called at the house of old friends across the road and it was most embarrassing to them and us that the fire-irons and fireside rug from our front room now adorned their fireplace! We left quickly. We then saw the father of the family who had been in our shelter. He crossed the road and hurried by. When we enquired of the salvage men who were working in the road if they could get round into the shelter they said it had been cleared out by the people who were in there. Looking back all these years later I suppose it was sensible to use what seemed to be abandoned, but my father, who was ultra-honest and law-abiding, felt that this was a great betrayal and never got over it. We got our old piano, a couple of chairs, an armchair and a tin bath of knick-knacks put into store for the duration. For the rest of our home, he claimed the princely sum of £30 as reparations at the end of the war.

JOAN HERRING

HUNTER'S MOON

The moon hangs like a shining silver disc
In a cloudless sky,
Shedding brilliant light on the ground below.
A hunter's moon.

The bombers come, droning through the night,
Casting their shadows ahead in grim warning.
People huddle in shelters underground,
Helpless and afraid of the violence to come.

The sound of heavy gunfire fills the air,
And the ground shakes with the blast of bombs.
Falling masonry sends up clouds of dust
Which hide the devastation for a moment.

There is an eerie silence now, the bombers gone,
Fear fades away and sleep comes at last.
But under the cloudless sky, among ruined homes,
The dead and dying lie broken in the moonlight.

DOROTHY BARTON

ONE SATURDAY AFTERNOON ...

Saturday, late afternoon, and an air-raid warning sounds. The target was the East India docks and the Royal Albert docks. Not very far away was the Woolwich Arsenal where they made and stored munitions.

Wave after wave of enemy planes came over at short intervals for hours and hours. The warehouses along the riverside were stocked with a lot of tinned food. Once the bombs dropped, the tins got hot, expanded and exploded. It was as though fireworks had been released, with tins everywhere, even flying through the air and very dangerous. Once it got dark it seemed that the whole of London was on fire.

The next morning, in a state of shock we took a walk round the houses. It was as though there had been an earthquake. Beds were hanging from bedroom floors, broken glass, bricks, rubble and thick dust everywhere. There was a funny sort of quietness, almost as though you were in another world, not real.

During the morning lots of heavy rescue squads and air-raid wardens were busy sorting out debris in the hope of finding any one still alive.

Not long after this came incendiary bombs, usually several at a time. They dropped as though in a basket and opened up and covered quite a large area. We all had a bucket of sand which was kept at the ready and if one of these bombs dropped on your roof there was a chance that you could put the fire out before it took hold. We had lots of wardens all working on our behalf, and the amount of hours they worked was tremendous.

Sometimes there would be a whole street on fire, and this took a lot of controlling, especially bearing in mind that bombs would still be dropping. It was just frightening and awful; not a pleasant time to look back on.

LILIAN BURNETT

THE ARMY HOP

We didn't give "squatters' rights" a thought (or even realise they existed). During World War II, Blackheath was almost deserted. Most of its population had rushed "north of Watford" or elsewhere away from this bombing zone.Thus many of the large houses stood empty. The Paragon, an elegant, fashionable Georgian crescent overlooking the Heath, had had its quota of bombing but some of the houses had escaped, and were unoccupied.

We found the large ground-floor room of a fairly safe house (if any building could be described as safe, with destruction about to descend from the skies, sometimes without warning) to have a small informal club. Outside each of these mansion-like buildings, there was a "mounting block" or stone in order that the affluent might have less difficulty in climbing into their carriages. We were young then, and these reminders of the past were of little consequence to us. We had by then had a year or so of war, and had been conditioned to think only of the present. The future for us was to draw "a blank" on a "ticket" – this was the language – if your ticket was on a bomb, you'd had it, and it was the next world for you. There was nothing whatsoever to be done about it. So we decided that in whatever form and in whatever time was available to us, we would indulge in some of the joys of our youthful existence. So we moved in.

Someone produced a 78 rmp gramophone, and we pooled our records, a collection of musical comedies of the '20s and '30s, songs of World War I such as "If You Were the Only Girl in the World", "Pack up Your Troubles", etc., music from "The Merry Widow", and "The Quaker Girl", also a much treasured and much played record of Tchaikovsky's "Sleeping Beauty", and of course, the music of Novello and Coward.

The main services had been turned off for safety, so we brought flasks of hot water and contributed if we could (as food rationing was a part of our lives) tea, sugar, etc. Our membership (and it proved to be most valuable for our stores) included some of the Armed Forces who had to man the anti-aircraft battery on the Heath, which included a mobile gun. We asked no questions about the stores, so we had no answers, as there were posters everywhere warning that "Walls have Ears".

Often our military friends had to make a speedy exit as an Air Raid Warning sounded, "Wailing Winnie" as it was called. We shot down into the basement where we had made an air-raid shelter, reinforced with sandbags. It was a case of waiting for the glorious sound of the all-clear.

Club activities included a record evening which very often led to a sing-song. We danced too – foxtrots, waltzes, the Veleta and the Military Two Step. One of the club members had trained at the Royal Ballet School (but was directed for war work of some clerical nature). She really put us through our paces. We learnt a form of the Lambeth Walk and the Park Parade. This dance must have been her own invention, but unfortunately she has since died and the secret must have died too. We also invented the "Army Hop". This varied on each occasion and was made up as we went along.

Our friends from the Heath had to be ready for action at any minute, so had to dance in their Army boots. It's a miracle that many of us weren't crippled as there were many dancers with two left feet.

Remember too, we had no electricity, only a storm lantern and, of course, we had to keep the black-out rules. Many a time there was an aerial dog-fight overhead and bombs falling all around. We would all be ready to help if this was possible.

It could well be said that we were "tempting providence" by having this club, although it's possible it was one of the war's best kept secrets. Often many of us didn't have time to visit the club for weeks on end as our various war duties kept us very busy indeed. When we were there we were possibly as safe as anywhere. There was a Warden's Post around the corner in Morden Road. The wardens knew of our existence, and in fact often looked in for a chat or maybe for an hour or so to relax. We were all issued with tin hats, a more practical "hand-out" for everyone than gas masks.

VIVIEN PRINCE

ALARMS AND FALSE ALARMS

I am sure that no one in the South East of England in the dark and dangerous days of late 1940 and early 1941 could ever forget the constant fear of the wailing siren, bright blue sky streaked with tracer bullet smoke, solemn barrage balloons bobbing about like droopy elephants on a long string, and the wave after wave attacks from the wonderful Spitfires, and the sky dotted with bright red bursts of ack-ack gunfire.

We watched as planes were hit and nose dived to earth with a high pitched whine, black smoke pouring from their tails, and we cheered every time it was an enemy bomber or Messerschmidt, sometimes seeing the crew drifting down safely by parachute. I have felt remorse since then that we gave no heed to the fact that lives were being lost. They were the enemy and it was them or us.

In September 1940 I was working near Eltham Church as cashier in a radio shop, and each time the siren went, my manager shut the shop and went home to his family shelter. It was not big enough for me or the shop boy, so I could either go to the basement of Burtons shop or try to get home. I considered the Burtons corner to be a vulnerable target on the cross roads, and I feared being trapped under a large building, so I used to run home.

Each time I heard bombs falling, I lay on the ground, the Air Raid Warden shouting to me to "take cover", then ran breathlessly to my home. The front door was always left open for anyone to take cover if needed. I'd dash straight through and into the shelter. When the all-clear sounded I went back to work. I don't recall how many times I did this, but it was quite a few.

I could see from the shop towards Woolwich as the sky became black with smoke from fires started along the entire length of the river. As dusk fell, the black turned to an ominous red. I remember people going home that evening solemnly looking towards the glow and remarking that we would have a bad night when the bombers returned. And of course we did, and for many nights and days to follow.

My father drove a tram between Eltham and Abbey Wood and was expected home about eight o'clock in the evening. Mum and I huddled together in the shelter all night, afraid and worried as Dad had not returned.

When dawn came, and a brief spell of quiet, I went to Well Hall Road to try to get some news. I was amazed to see hundreds of people walking along the road from the direction of Woolwich, weary and solemn, workers from the Arsenal, the docks and local factories, unable to get home from the previous day's work and having been in shelters all night. I saw a transport inspector and asked for news of my father. He was very agitated as three trams were missing and he could not get any information. Fortunately someone recognized me and told me Dad was in Woolwich. The roads were closed by hose pipes and he would not leave the tram, which was his responsibility, until relief arrived. That was not until the next morning. Men and girls of London Transport did a grand job in those dark days, helping London to "Carry On".

There were always incidents that brought humour to those terrifying times, and one concerned my mother. She took it on herself to remain alert, never getting into nightclothes throughout the blitz, to enable Dad and me to snatch a little sleep knowing she was keeping watch and would alert us of approaching raids. When enemy aircraft approached Kent the radio went off so that was the first warning.

One particularly bad night was slowly giving way to dawn, when Mum said "All Clear" and we staggered sleepily up the garden and indoors, collapsing in chairs to try to get a bit of rest. After a short while she suddenly said "Siren" and out we went again, Mum calling neighbours each side. "Come on, air raid," and all three occupants of adjoining homes returned to the shelter, and there we stayed, and stayed on and on, remarking it *was* rather quiet, when the wail started again and Mum called "All Clear", until our next door husband said, "No, it is the warning" and the gun fire began noisily.

She must have dozed off and missed the first "all-clear", taking us all indoors on the next warning and calling everyone out on the all-clear! Not popular, as it was very damp and cold in the early morning in a hole dug in the earth.

The autumn months of 1940 were extremely wet, resulting in overnight flooding of Anderson shelters. Our suitcase containing the family treasures, Dad's World War I medals, policies and precious childhood photographs floated out and the contents came to rest scattered up the garden path.

To make the next best protection possible, we tilted the settee in the living room on to the side of the table, and did the same at the ends with the arm chairs. On the table top we piled mattresses and blankets to take any flying glass or debris, and then we all crawled under the table every night in very cramped conditions. It was in November 1940 that I met my future husband and his first introduction to our home was to join us "under the kitchen table" when the warning sounded, and so stayed with us all night!

JOYCE MILAN

A FLYING VISIT

I was living on the South Coast throughout the "phoney war", Dunkirk and the Blitz and although we had air raid warnings when the German bombers were passing overhead, we weren't a target and only collected a few stray bombs unloaded by them on their way home. We did see plenty of vapour trails in the sky in September 1940 and watched dog-fights over our gardens, but it was nothing like the terrible experience of London or Coventry or even "Bomb Alley" in Kent.

My eldest brother and his wife were living in Ilford with their small baby and he worked in the City. They came to stay with us for Christmas and when my brother went back to his office in London Wall after the holiday, he found the whole area had been reduced to rubble. The office safe was still intact but the heat of the fires had been so intense that everything inside it was shrivelled. At the beginning of the war he had advised my mother to let him put the deeds of our house into that safe "for safety" and he brought them back to her. They were on vellum and had shrunk to the size of a dog's bone – completely impossible to open or restore to their original size.

Not realising just how devastating an air raid could be, I arranged to stay with my brother for a weekend. I was at Liverpool Street Station when the warning sounded, but I decided to board my train because it was the last one that night. It was a stupid thing to do. I was (not surprisingly) alone in the carriage with a grandstand view of tracer bullets going up and bombs and shrapnel coming down. There were searchlights criss-crossing the sky. The train crawled at a walking pace and I sat, petrified, in what seemed to me as flimsy as a matchbox. Eventually, after a very long time, we reached Ilford station and there we had to wait for hours in the booking hall until the all-clear was given.

My brother lived some distance from the station and normally I would have taken a bus, but there weren't any running, so I had no option but to walk. My legs were like jelly but I carried on through the deserted streets (no street lamps and very eerie, but there was a moon) and at last I was at my brother's flat.

Next morning when we ventured out we found the whole area where I had walked the night before was cordoned off – it was riddled with unexploded bombs. I have the greatest admiration for the people of London whose amazing courage and cheerfulness under the most terrifying bombardment contributed in no small measure to the final outcome of the war. If the people of London had broken under the strain, not even the magnificent "Few" could have saved Britain from defeat.

GWEN PARRISH

Londoners take shelter in an Underground Station.

DAILY ROUTINES

The nightly raids continued. We all slept in the dining room, with the exception of my mother. She was very nervous and was offered a place in our next door neighbour's Morrison. My father, three brothers and myself played paper games (usually Battleships and Cruisers) and cards, shouting "Duck" when we heard the bombs coming down. On one occasion my brother got stuck under the bed and we had to yank him out. The bombs came down in sticks of five, and we used to count them. We soon got to feel in which direction they were falling, and there was this awful "whoosh" followed by the crunch of the bombs exploding. Sometimes, after the all-clear and the cup of tea which I think most people made afterwards, my eighteen-year-old brother and I would put a coat on top of our pyjamas, and walk round the local streets. The smell of smoke and cordite, and the sight often of broken water mains and precious water running down the roads are still clear in my mind.

A week after the Blitz started, my mother and younger twelve-year-old brother were evacuated and my father was compelled to sleep at Millbank as he was on shift duties and travelling was difficult. That left two of my brothers and myself. Our parents were not too happy about our staying in the house, so arrangements were made for us to share the air raid shelter of the local warden, who didn't use the shelter herself, but two of her brothers-in-law did. The men folk slept on a mattress on the floor, whilst I was given two chairs by the entrance. I spent most of the night in a foetal position, it is a wonder I didn't end up with curvature of the spine! One of the men was very nervous, and insisted on the door of the shelter being kept closed, and as they were heavy smokers, the atmosphere became claustrophobic. He was also a loud snorer. Personally I would have preferred to take a chance in our own house, but I had made a firm promise. A bucket was put outside the door to collect the shrapnel!! There would be the arguments. "That's one of ours", was known as "famous last words".

We used to stagger out of the shelter in the early hours. If the all-clear came early enough we could sometimes stretch out on our own beds for an hour or so before getting up.

There was a routine of day to day living. One would breakfast, complete as many household tasks as possible in the time available, then make one's way to work. The Electric Light Company initially took over the church hall near Hornimans Gardens, then later a large house in Beckenham. One would invariably have to walk to work, as buses were diverted due to bomb damage on the roads, and few and far between. Our task at the time was to create some sort of order out of the boxes and crates of papers that had been salvaged, a very boring and laborious task, dirty too. It was remarkable that eventually there were fewer than a hundred accounts missing. The journey home was usually on shanks's pony, although sometimes we would get a lift, on one occasion in a Black Maria!

On arrival home it would be a scratch meal, then prepare for the shelter. One would wash, clean one's teeth, and I would pin my hair up and tie a turban around my head. Black-out would be secured, kettles and saucepans filled with water in case the mains were damaged in the night, get the cat in (if we could find him). Then whatever time was left was spent in getting clothes, etc., ready for work next morning, and any other jobs needing doing until the air raid warning sounded.

What I cannot recall is, what did we eat? When did I do the shopping? And the laundry? My memory fails me in this respect. We had no "fridges" in those days, although my mother had a well stocked stores cupboard. I can only assume we raided this.

One incident in this area I do recall. It was later on in the month, when there was only my eighteen-year-old brother left at home, as the younger one had been evacuated to Surbiton with his firm and I had been down to Rotherfield for a couple of days where my mother was evacuated. I was gradually taking clothes down for her and my young brother, so the eighteen-year-old was fending for himself. When I arrived home it seemed he had been living on boiled rice and sultanas, and had used every saucepan in the process! I was faced with the task of scouring burnt rice off them all.

We used to go down to Kent most week-ends (travelling by Green Line coach), and the best part of this was being able to soak in a bath.

Standards on the whole were maintained, I remember the girls at the office all arrived looking spick and span, hair carefully styled, faces made up. One girl had a mass of curls (pin-curls) which must have taken her ages to set. It was important for our morale not to let things slide. By early October, my eighteen year old brother had received his calling up papers for the R.A.F. and it was decreed that no way could I stay in the home alone. I must admit I wasn't keen, as, although I often moaned about the work they caused, I would have missed the company of my brothers very much. By mid October we were all split up, my father being the only one to remain in London.

MARGARET KIPPIN

London Underground Station. November, 1940.

IN A PICKLE

I was in London at the start of the Blitz. Nights were spent in the public shelter. We didn't wait for the siren, but went down long before to settle into our places. Ours were by the latrine buckets! Two bunk beds made of iron ran along the side of the wall. We brought our bedding with us. My stepmother also had with her a large bag containing food, drink and her marriage lines, insurance policies, etc. We didn't see my father from one day to the next as he was in the A.F.S. fighting fires in the heart of London.

I always took books with me, but sometimes I couldn't concentrate on reading because of the smell from the buckets. And with so many people in the confined space there was constant noise, it always seemed a long time before people fell asleep, and then it seemed they slept lightly.

You couldn't hear much of what was happening outside. The only time you heard bombs falling was when they fell very nearby, like the time the pickle factory got bombed at the top of the road. The shelter was about half way down the road, but still brick dust and the smell of cordite came in, and we heard the glass breaking, and the smell of vinegar and spice was over-powering. My stepmother and I were worried because our house was only three doors away from the factory.

In the morning, after a sleepless night, we came out to find we had no glass in the windows, there were onions and slates in our small front garden and inside the front-room on the settee there was glass and gherkins and onions all mixed up together.

My stepmother promptly got a bowl and said, "Waste not, want not!", and we set about collecting up the onions to wash them. We had onions to eat after that for weeks. Of course we children in the street had great fun pelting each other with squashed onions as they were everywhere.

MARGARET PHAIR

SHOPPING IN THE BLITZ

When the air raid sirens went, you sometimes went into a shelter with strangers. You'd perhaps never seen any of these people before, and they'd all bring bits and pieces with them, it was more like a tea party, sharing whatever you had. They'd been queueing up for that all day, but nobody minded because they thought, "Well we could be here today and gone tomorrow."

The word would get round, one would tell the other, "Mrs. White, she's got some tinned fruit in", and she'd get a nice long queue outside her shop. You'd all get one tin each; and of course they'd send the children as well. A tin of fruit was a real luxury and so you didn't mind waiting for it. And the people were so kind, they were taking it and then sharing it out, especially when you knew there were children there that never had anything. People would hear that so and so was really hard up and they'd think, "What a shame! Oh, let her have some of mine."

We had to queue for the whale meat for our dog Gyp. My dad got to hear of a butchers at the Elephant and Castle where they sold whale meat. It was like steak, and Gyp liked that. You'd really think it was steak. You didn't pay coupons for that. It was off ration. If you were lucky the butcher would give you a bone. You'd ask for a bone for the dog, but Gyp didn't often get the bone, because Mum used to make stews with that. I think Mum did manage to get a bit of pork for Christmas. She'd gradually save her coupons. Now and then she'd kill off one of the chickens, because it was hard to find food for them. Often she would share them out with other people, especially poor people who hadn't got much.

ELLEN CLARK

OUR LIVES WERE CONTROLLED BY THE BLITZ

My fiance and I decided to get married in the March of 1940, and we had a nice wedding at St. Alfege's Church in Greenwich. He had tried to get into the Air Force, but had been turned down as he was short-sighted. So he went into the Civil Defence, driving an ambulance, and I was on war work at Siemens.

When my husband was on night duty, I would stay with my mother-in-law. Unfortunately she lived on the top storey of a block of flats, so when the warning went, most evenings we had to pick up our bedding and get down to the shelter in the courtyard, and stay there all night. We would watch the searchlights, from the Territorial Army on Blackheath, and from the soldiers on Woolwich Common.

Our lives were controlled by the Blitz. At the end of the first year we were bombed out, and lost most of our wedding presents. We moved to East Greenwich to a flat over the Maypole Dairies. Underneath the shops there were shelters, and at about six o'clock in the evening, everyone living in that area went down, and spent the night there. People were very friendly, and there would be music and singing to try and forget the raids outside. We cheered when the all-clear went.

One day, a bomb dropped in Greenwich and all the tram lines were damaged, so the people who worked in London had to go by boat on the Thames. My father was a seaman for the Port of London, and once his pier was nearly hit by a bomb, and he found himself floating in the middle of the Thames.

We were lucky because seamen had extra rations for food and clothing coupons. We had to line up for luxuries like oranges and bananas. Your neighbour would come and tell you where the fruit was and we would line up for hours, to get some.

When I was pregnant, I reluctantly evacuated to a mansion in the countryside owned by a Lady Paget. It was a small village, so you can imagine the looks we got as we climbed out of the coach – an invasion of thirty very pregnant women! A few weeks later I had a daughter, Brenda. We heard nothing of the bombing down there; only the planes going over.

Eventually, I was homesick, so I returned to Greenwich. Brenda was not a good baby, she cried night and day, but we put this down to her being a war baby. We had to keep picking her up and running to the shelters. Anyway, life went on, and we are lucky to be here to tell our stories.

ELSIE LEHANE

Cockney humour and the "carry-on" spirit during the "Blitz".
September, 1940.

"WHERE DID YOU GET THAT DRESS?"

My sister got married during the war, and that was another kerfuffle. You couldn't get cake or anything, and all the dried fruit was on coupons. So what you did, you exchanged. Say you knew somebody who liked tea, you'd give them your tea coupons. I remember, we were collecting fruit for ages because you got so much every so often. In the end she did get a nice wedding cake made all in squares.

And as for the wedding dress, she had to borrow one because buying a wedding dress would really cost you. Actually, I think half of Blackheath must have borrowed this dress. It was a really lovely Victorian one with this lovely big hoop round. People would take it to the cleaners and some would take the hoop out, and they'd treat the person they borrowed it from, they'd buy her something. It went from one to the other. It did a really good turn that dress and it seemed to fit so many people, which was marvellous really. Everybody that saw the wedding photos said, "Gosh, where did you get your dress?" And my sister would say, "Oh, you can borrow it."

ELLEN CLARK

39

BLOWN FROM FRONT TO BACK

In 1940 when I was a child of eleven, we lived in Bexley Village with a garden backing on to the River Cray. Mum used to leave me and my baby sister to sleep in the Anderson shelter at the top of the garden near the house while she went firewatching. On the night in question, we were alone in the shelter, except for the dog. He was a black pomeranian, and he was always down the shelter before the siren went. He was always the first one down when there was a warning. Normally there would have been two of our neighbours sharing the Anderson, because theirs was flooded. But they never got down there that time because it was a very short warning.

We had a little old man, a Mr. Johnson staying with us who was the verger at St. Mary's church. He'd been bombed out of his place and had to stay with us in the spare room. Mr. Johnson wouldn't come down to the shelter. He used to sit up there in the house.

Well, this night, we had three high explosives came and landed, one in the road, one right at the bottom of our garden. And I remember we had a clock down in the shelter, and it went, doing-doing-doing, flying round the walls. There was no light down there at all. I was petrified.

The green houses and the sheds that were down the bottom of the garden all blew up towards the back of the house when the bomb landed, and everything fell on top of our shelter. The Anderson shelter was buried, but it was all right. A lot of the debris fell across the shelter door.

When my mother came back from fire-watching, she realised the bomb had landed down our end of the street, and she ran round to the back garden. She and the neighbours in the next shelter got us out. If we hadn't been down the shelter we'd've been killed.

We had no garden left and the back of our house was gone. The kitchen was completely wrecked except for the old fashioned dresser which was attached to the wall. Every plate on it was broken, but all the cups were still hanging in a neat row on their handles.

When they'd got us out of the shelter, we all went looking for Mr. Johnson. He was in the front room. He'd been sitting by the door at the kitchen table doing his books and his paper work, and the blast just took him. It was one of those walk through houses – he'd been blown from the back to the front. He'd gone through three doors. He was on his knees looking for his glasses in the front room.

Salvaging valued possessions from a bombed house, 18.10.40.

We were sent to my gran's at Sevenoaks. The bomb damage people came in and they removed everything in sight. That included a lot of our personal belongings which we never saw again.

BABS DOWNES

A LUCKY ESCAPE

I was seventeen when the war started, and I worked at Siemens, the big munitions factory in Charlton. Our house backed right on to the factory so we were a target for the bombers. Sometimes we were just going to sit down to our dinner and the siren'd go. We'd take the dinner with us down the shelter. We always had a bag ready with all our valuables in, and we'd take them down too. It was funny really that we'd go to work nicely dressed, then we'd come home and put on an old jumper and slacks and go down the shelter, leaving all our best clothes in the house. Looking back we thought what fools we were! However, we did take all our valuables with us; rings, jewellery and money – we always had them by the side of us.

The Anderson shelter was at the top of the garden. Some nights we'd get a good night there, other nights, no sleep at all. One night it was very quiet and so towards morning I said to my mother, "Can we go to bed now, Mum?" So she said, "Yes, I think we will. We'll go up to the house." There was only my younger brother and me with Mum and Dad, because the other six brothers and sisters were all in the Forces.

Mum and Dad had a bed on the floor downstairs. My younger brother and I went upstairs to bed. The next thing I knew, I heard a great thud (I didn't know what it was) and when I looked, gosh! we'd only got half a room left. I was still half asleep when the air-raid wardens came dashing up the stairs and grabbed us. As they took us down, the stairs just caved right in behind us. I was saying, "Put me down, put me down. I've got no clothes on." He said, "You're alright, you're alright." I found this old coat that was in the hall, and got that round me. My younger brother was half asleep and half awake, the same as I was. They took us to the London Mission Hall up the road. We just sat there in a daze, and gradually other people were brought in, some of them crying. They gave us tea, and a W.V.S. lady gave me some more clothes, because I was still in my nightie. I know my hair was all matted with oil and grease and I had to have most of it cut off. I must've looked pretty!

Gradually the people got us talking and brought us out of shock. I think they were trained to do that. Two or three hours later, the air raid wardens came in and said, "Don't you realise how lucky you are? You're the only four that's still alive." They said that if my brother had got out of his bed on the other side, he'd have gone down into a crater.

Nine people had been killed in the blast. It was a landmine which was meant for Siemens, not for our houses. There was no fire, just a massive explosion. In one house, the mother and sister were killed, but the baby who was right down in the basement, survived. The father was out fire-watching, so at least the baby did still have a father. We had such a lucky escape. I felt it was all my

fault in a way, as it had been my bright idea to leave the shelter and go back to the house.

We only stayed in the Mission Hall for a few hours. We went back to the house in the morning to see if anything had survived but it was all rubble. Anyway, I can remember the W.V.S. van coming down the road, giving tea and sandwiches to the other people who lived across the way and who had also experienced some of the blast. And of course all the power was off. Then the undertakers came down, and I could see them with these long black coffins, which wasn't very nice, and we had to see all that.

The marvellous thing was that Gyp, our black and white dog, came out alive. He was smothered in dust and dirt, but he came out all right. Then two or three days later someone came and told my mother that they'd found our rabbit as well. His cage was all crushed underneath the rubble, but he was all right. My mother was pleased, but she was upset as well because she didn't have anywhere to keep him. The warden said, "Oh could I have him?" So Mum said, "Yes, but don't say anything to the children. And promise you won't kill him or eat him or anything?" The warden said, "Ooh, no, no, I wouldn't. This is a one off." She didn't tell us until a long while after, because she knew that we would want to keep him. So this air raid warden had him, and I know he kept him.

My parents had gone up to the Town Hall to be allocated some money, because of course they had lost everything. They would have offered us a house to stay in, but we were very lucky in that we had my sister's house in Greenwich to go to. We were looking after it for her at the time because she had evacuated to Cornwall with her two girls and her husband was away in the army.

But my father had been badly shaken by the explosion and he said there was no way he was ever going to stay in a house again. He was taking us all off to Chislehurst Caves. Oh, it was horrible there, all damp and chalky. We went every night regular, as soon as my father came home. We'd come home from work, see that the dog was all right, we'd feed him and everything, before we went to the Caves. Then we'd say, "Now be a good boy, Gyp. You stay here tonight." But the dog kept running back from that house to our old house in Charlton. He'd just put his foot through the anti-blast paper on the windows, climb out and run back home again. So at the finish we took him to the caves with us as well. He didn't really like it down there. He was like me, he couldn't wait to get out.

I suppose there must have been some bedding arrangement, because I'm sure my mother wouldn't have let us lie on damp floors. I think there were wooden slats and you made up a bed for yourself on those. We had to get up very early in the morning to get to work from there by seven o'clock.

Well, we did that for quite a few months. Then my mother, my brother and I put our heads together, and we said, "Look Dad, we could get killed travelling up to New Cross and back to Chislehurst Caves through all the raids." But Dad didn't agree. He said, "Oh well, I'll go on my own then." He'd really lost his nerve, he couldn't help it. Well, my brother felt a bit sad to think of my dad going to the caves on his own, so he went with him for a while, but soon he got fed up, and at the finish my poor dad had to go out to the caves on his own. My mother, my brother and I stayed at my sister's house in Greenwich.

Dad made friends with several people in the caves, and he would come home and tell us different stories. He was always coming back with other people's hard luck stories. He'd say to Mum, "There's this poor soul all on his own, and he doesn't get what I get", and so on and so on. So Mum would finish up making extra food parcels for him to take with him!

ELLEN CLARK

A tin hatted postman making his rounds in a bombed area of London.
Letters addressed to wrecked houses are marked accordingly and returned.
10th October 1940.

DELIVERIES

Deliveries of milk and bread were made as usual, in spite of air raids, by horse drawn vans. The horses had to be taken out of the shafts and tethered to a tree or lamp post during a raid, otherwise they would bolt with fear and cause damage to themselves and others.

Postal deliveries were regular and very good. Daily papers were printed and distributed without fail. Telegrams were dreaded and they generally contained bad news. Armed Service casualties were notified by telegram, delivered by boy cyclists with pill box caps.

EDIE McHARDY

DANCING THROUGH THE BLITZ

For social life, we didn't do too badly. We weren't far from the Woolwich barracks, and they used to have dances there nearly every Sunday afternoon, providing it was quiet. And on a Saturday evening as well, in Woolwich, there was usually a dance on.

When we went dancing, of course the troops would wear their big boots, but you didn't mind that really. You'd think, "Well we'll help them have a good time", because you didn't know how long it would be before they would go away. Sometimes you'd go shopping in Woolwich, and you'd see all the girlfriends waving goodbye to their boyfriends or husbands who were all being marched off to the station. That was sad. I didn't like to see that. Especially if we'd seen them as well and been to the dance with them.

Although it was black-out you found your way. You'd just take a torch with you to get up and down the kerbs. It wasn't a bit frightening to go out in the dark. Everybody would call out, "Hi there! Had a good time?" and that was that. You could be coming home from a dance then and the siren would go. Naturally you'd go into the first shelter you could find. And everybody would mix in, and talk about where they'd been. I never thought that I would get killed or anything like that.

ELLEN CLARK

A SHELTERED LIFE!

I returned home from evacuation in the early months of 1941 at the age of fourteen-and-a-half years to start work. By this time the air raids on London had become less frequent, and we would enjoy several nights in a row without an air raid. The atmosphere became much more relaxed, the enjoyment of trouble-free unbroken nights' sleep did wonders for our morale.

I lived with my parents and four brothers on an estate of flats. Two or three surface brick-built air raid shelters had been built on the lawns in front of each block, and the ground between them was dug up for the tenants to grow vegetables, etc. The shelters, fitted out with wooden bunks, were allocated so that no-one had more than a few yards to walk from the block entrances.

At this time only four of our family of seven were at home, more often than not only three as my father who was in the A.F.S. spent most of his nights at the fire station. Even when not on duty, he wouldn't stay in the shelter during an air raid.

The practice of going to the shelter every night had stopped when the raids became less regular and we only went when the siren had sounded and the raid was likely to be prolonged and close. We lived on the top floor of the flats and were reluctant to troop downstairs for nuisance raids, or fake alarms. From our windows we could see for miles across London, and often we could judge approximately what part of London was "getting it" and the severity of the raid.

Occasionally we got caught out by a raid that seemed a long way off suddenly moving towards us. Then there was a rush downstairs to the shelter. On one occasion we were watching an object in the sky which appeared to be drifting. We argued for some seconds whether it was going up or down, or whether it was near, or far. Almost too late to get clear of the windows, we realised it was a land mine which exploded some streets away. We were lucky to escape any damage.

The nights we spent in the shelter were usually quite communal affairs, especially if it was noisy, with occasional sing-songs, playing games etc., until it was time to settle down to try and sleep. We had to keep our ears tuned to the sound of incendiary bombs falling so that we could put them out before they did any lasting damage. The sound of the anti-aircraft guns was frightening and it took time to convince yourself that they were helping to keep the bombers away.

Coming from a family of all boys, it was my first experience of having to share accommodation with girls! One of the girls was later to join the Windmill Theatre chorus line and a few years afterwards, when I was in the Forces, she was one of our pin-ups. That gave me a talking point!

The morning after a heavy raid was a daunting experience because most of us had to carry on with our normal lives. I had just started work as a boy messenger for the G.P.O. in central London. We were still expected to be on time for work, with our uniforms clean, belt and buttons polished. The only concession was that we were issued with steel helmets. I travelled by tram from Brixton and often it meant picking my way through rubble, climbing over hoses and being diverted due to unexploded bombs. Sometimes I found no trams were running which meant a long walk.

On arrival at the office I was faced with more walking to deliver telegrams etc. There was always the hope that the next night would be quiet and the trams would be running.

BILL HERRING

EMERGENCY WASHING SERVICE

Washing is brought to the National Emergency Washing Service Van, where it is marked and sorted by the supervisor. It then goes into the van, where the trained staff wash, dry and iron the bundle. No charge is made for this washing service.

COOKING FOR THE AMBULANCE DRIVERS

I was a cook in an ambulance station during the Blitz. I was twenty-four when I worked there, and recently married. I applied for the job myself, even though I'd had no experience. I just took a chance but of course they were desperate for staff. Before that, I'd worked in the Perga Milk Carton Factory, but I had to leave that job because the factory closed down. There was a German governor there who went back to Germany at the start of the war.

As I said, I'd had no previous experience except what I'd picked up from my mum. They asked me if I could cook and I said yes. There was one cook in the morning and one in the afternoon. We did two hot meals a day. I had to cook for about forty people on a shift. The only thing I did wrong was I didn't cook enough at first, but I soon learned.

We'd vary the meals from day to day. We couldn't give them the same two days running. They had really good food there, things like steak and kidney pie, liver and bacon casserole, braising steak and roast. They said I was good. The other cook was no good – her gravy was like thick Bisto. They used to grumble about her cooking. Her greens used to be stewed and stewed and stewed. They wanted me to take a diploma and then go round other ambulance stations in London supervising the cooks. I didn't do it, but I must've been good, though I say it myself.

The dinner had to be ready at one o'clock, but of course if the ambulance drivers were out after a raid you had to give it to them when they came in. Sometimes they were called out in the middle of their dinner, and then they just had to run.

There were a lot of well-to-do ladies working there, and some of them were getting on in years. They were voluntary workers in the Auxiliary Ambulance Service. We were Station 144, Shardeloes Road.

The manager was a nice fellow, Don Carpenter. He did all the ordering and buying of the food – he was in charge of the canteen. We were in charge of the washing up and laying the tables as well as the cooking. Once they'd had the meals you cleared away and you washed up. We weren't cooking all the time, it wasn't like in a cafe – we just did one big batch. We had no helpers for the washing up, we did the whole lot on your own.

There was a fellow there, who used to call me his little pigeon and we used to have a little cuddle every morning or afternoon when he saw me. His wife didn't mind. She was called Aggie and she worked there as well. We had our fun there, it wasn't all sad.

I used to walk from Forest Hill to New Cross every day to get to work. The shifts were six in the morning till two, then two till ten. I used to walk around with my tin helmet on. I had to walk home in the dark at ten o'clock. When I was expecting, I had morning sickness and I used to be sick over everybody's privet hedge. I worked there from 1939-1943, and then I had to stop because I was six months pregnant. It was good working there. We were all happy. Everybody was happy.

ELSIE HOUSE

AN UNDESERVED SOAKING

It didn't take us long to get used to sleeping at night in the shelter, once the blitz got under way. I never enjoyed the rude awakening of the air raid siren, nor did I like the feel of cold shoes without socks on my feet. An overcoat was kept across the foot of my bed, and scrambled into. With gas-mask slung over my shoulder I joined everyone else in the rush to comparative safety.

One night, the raid had gone on as usual until the early hours, and it was with a huge sigh of relief that we welcomed the "all-clear". Wearily we staggered back to bed. I was in a deep sleep when all of a sudden a bucket of cold water landed on me. I shot up in bed, and there grinning at me from his ladder was an air raid warden. He was full of apologies, but said that during the night an incendiary bomb had landed in the gutter right above my window. When he chucked the bucket of water over the bomb he had failed to notice my window was open, and most of it shot through on to me. Well, that was his story!

In the early part of the Blitz, people were paid compensation for loss of furniture during bombing. You filled in a form, submitted it to a government official, and eventually got paid out. It wasn't long before certain fiddles took place, such as people claiming for expensive carpets and furniture they didn't have. In the end the compensation was stopped.

Once the blitz started in earnest, we got into the habit of letting Mother know exactly where we were during the day. I remember the one occasion I didn't. It worried me so much I never did it again. I left my own school in the morning to do cookery lessons in another school that luckily had all the facilities. During the lunch break I realised this school was in the vicinity of my aunt's home. I calculated that if I ran as a crow flies, I could spend a short time with her, scrounge a bar of chocolate, and still be back in time for afternoon lessons. I hadn't thought of a possible air raid.

Shortly after I started out the dreaded siren wailed. I had made up my mind to go to my aunt's and to my aunt's I would go, so I ran on. My shoes made a loud tapping in the quickly deserted streets. I raced down a very posh street. Lovely houses one side, on the other a small park, covered thickly with trees. Suddenly a hand grabbed me. I was hustled down some steps, and made to wait inside a maze of white-washed passages beneath the park. Luckily the raid turned out to be a false alarm. As soon as the all-clear sounded I was on my way to my aunt's once more, and determined to get there after all the effort I'd put in. She was certainly surprised, and I believe pleased, as I came away with my chocolate. Only later did I realise that in the event of a proper raid no one would have known where I was, and in case of a disaster I would have been one of the "unaccounted for".

MILLY GARDNER

IN THE THICK OF IT

I was approaching my 17th birthday. My three sisters were evacuated to Wales and Norfolk, leaving me with my mother and father to dive into the Anderson shelter when the sirens blasted out their warning of approaching aircraft.

I hated the shelter. It was so small, I felt as though I could not breathe, and to see my father leaping out with the pail of water and stirrup pump to put out incendiary bombs that had dropped in our street was so frightening, and then the waiting for his return. There were hundreds of these bombs dropped, along with screaming bombs and land mines.

My mother and I were visiting my father in St. Alfege's hospital, when we were told to go home quickly as a land mine was descending slowly on Blackwall Lane just yards from the hospital. It exploded with great devastation. It took us ages to get home to Charlton, walking most of the way.

The next day my father died. He was injured in the East India Docks as the bombs rained down. He was a policeman and he was patrolling along the dock side. He was a very nice father and was missed terribly.

The river Thames was like a silver snake to the German bombers and fighters as they met overhead. We watched many fights, with our R.A.F. boys weaving and diving, guns blasting away.

We lived next to Woolwich Barracks. The soldiers there had mobile guns mounted on huge lorries. As they moved around, sending their shells in the air, it was almost as if they were outside our shelter.

Going back to those silent monsters, the mines, I can remember these round objects descending very slowly on the end of a parachute. One did drop in the next road to us. After the terrific noise of bricks and masonry had quietened down, there came a cloud of white papers, which settled quickly on all our gardens. We thought they might have been propaganda leaflets, but as we picked them up, we realized they had come down from the many houses that had been gutted by the mine. They were family photographs which had been shredded by the bombing. It was so upsetting to look down on faces you knew, and then to wonder if they had escaped this weapon from Germany.

DORIS HOLLANDS

A WARTIME WEDDING

I had met my future husband in November 1940 during heavy air raids. He was in the Royal Navy on a gunnery course in Woolwich Arsenal from his base in Plymouth. We had discussed marriage and intended the wedding to be on September 11th (my mother and father's anniversary) and I still have that date marked in my diary for 1941 as "My Wedding".

However, this was not to be. On a weekend leave at the beginning of May, late on the Friday evening, we took a walk around the houses between air raid alerts, and he gave me the news that he was sailing on the Monday and we would have to be married at the weekend. The reason was that his mess in Plymouth had suffered a direct hit, demolishing the sleeping quarters and killing many Naval personnel. He had lost all his kit and even his best "tiddly" suit, so he borrowed one to be married in!

We returned home and broke the news to my mother and she said, "OK – we'll make it". Bearing in mind I was preparing for a wedding later, I had already bought bridal white satin, yards of turquoise taffeta (having cadged all my parents' and grandmother's clothing coupons – I even gave Grandma 2/6d for hers!) and a box of wedding invitations. We hastily wrote those out late that night and Mum went about posting them in neighbours' letter boxes and a few hurried ones in the post to relatives.

Saturday morning we visited the vicar for permission to marry, but for a special licence we had to apply to the parish church, where the reverend gentleman was very sick and met us in his pyjamas from his bed. The first question he asked was "Are you both over age?" It was twenty-one then, and of course we weren't, so both our parents' written consent was required. Although we knew his mother and father agreed, they were too frightened to come to London and the bombing, so we tried to get a message to them via the "local" that his father used, hoping he would call in there, this being in Yorkshire. He did get the message and sent a telegram say, "We give our consent".

We rushed back to the church, only to be told that this was not acceptable. It had to be in writing. I sat in that vestry in tears. I didn't know what to do, because in the meantime I had taken the white satin to a neighbour and she had begun to make the dress, taking it into the air raid shelter to sew. Also I said if she could manage to make the dresses, her two children could be bridesmaids. My next door neighbour was making her bridesmaids' dresses and my friend Irene had taken her material to her sister to make hers. I had been to Cuffs and bought my veil and head-dress, the local florist was making up the bouquets (the bridesmaids only had tulips and anemones, which I opened up to make them look like orchids) and the baker had a

Joyce Milan's wedding photo.

chocolate cake already made. Fruit was impossible to get and to make a wedding cake took months of collecting coupons for the ingredients.

My mother had pleaded with the grocer for a knuckle of bacon and used all the family rations for a little piece of beef. So with all this going on, I felt absolutely devastated when I returned home from the visit to the church. Then, through my tears, I looked out of the window late on the Saturday afternoon and saw a taxi draw up, and out came my "in laws". They had decided they *would* come, so we rushed Dad back to the Church immediately to sign the required form, paid fifteen shillings, and got the special licence. He was then able to have a cup of tea! We couldn't have any church music as the organist had been bombed out and the choir boys had been evacuated. Nor could we get cars to go to church. Petrol was very scarce and none of our friends owned cars, so we walked to church, my dad, me and four bridesmaids. It wasn't very far I admit, but it brought us a lot of attention.

After the ceremony we sat down to the wedding breakfast in Mum's only living room. She had borrowed chairs and trestles and we had the usual speeches. Immediately after, my in-laws left to get out of London before dusk and Irene went back to work. We assembled in the garden for a few "snaps", putting down a mat on the earth to make it look at bit "posh". The following day, Sunday, my husband and I went to the afternoon pictures in Lewisham and at five o'clock I saw him off at Well Hall Station and never saw him again for three years!

JOYCE MILAN

53

KEEPING GOING

TRAVELLING

Travelling in wartime in the blackout was rather difficult, to say the least. Signposts were blacked out, as were names on stations. This confused everybody, friend as well as the expected foe.

Trains were dimly lit with blue lighting and the blinds were kept down once it was dark, so between that and odd stops for no reason, it was very difficult to recognise one station from another even on familiar journeys. Long distance trains were always packed and passengers filled the corridors – they were of course steam trains. There were no refreshments available, but on most main line stations W.V.S. ladies and other voluntary groups were spread along the platforms handing out tea and food to travelling Service men and women – a welcome sight at all times of day and night.

One particular journey I remember was from Cardiff and the train had to stop outside Reading for some considerable time owing to a raid on London. When it finally started, it went very slowly with many stops. The railways were of course a target for bombers. Finally we reached Paddington and in the Underground there was the familiar sight of people settled in for the night's shelter. I felt an intruder, but the trains did not seem to disturb them.

When I got to Charing Cross there were no more trains to Charlton, so I got as far as New Cross where I hoped to get a tram. Whilst waiting at the stop, a van driver offered me a lift which I gratefully accepted. There was no fear of attack in those days and men were protective. He took me right to the door. He was probably as glad of some company as I was, and it got me home nice and quickly. Most journeys in those days were accompanied by the unexpected, not always pleasant but never boring.

EDIE McHARDY

A THRILLING FIND!

One night during the Blitz, there was a heavy raid and I said to my sister, Emily, "There's a big fire going on over Roman Road way. I want to go out and see if I can find a bit of shrapnel out there. I've wanted to find a good bit of shrapnel for ages, but I never manage it." My sister said, "Oh you and your shrapnel. Be careful how you go out there."

Well, I saw this bomb lying in the road. It was a proper bomb with fins on the end, and a nose and tail, and about a foot long. I didn't really know what to look for, and I thought it was dead, so I counted it as shrapnel, and didn't see any danger. In fact, I was absolutely thrilled with it and took it indoors.

"Look what I've got 'Em!", I said. She said, "Christ, it looks dangerous. Is it alive?" "Course it isn't", I said, "falling from that distance! How could it be? I'll put it out on the landing and I'm going out."

Well, it had been there a couple of weeks when my mother came to visit me. I showed it to her and she said, "Gawd! It looks like a bomb." I said, "I think it is, but I think it's gone off. I don't know." She said, "Ooh, this is interesting. Can I take it to work with me?" She worked in a big factory banging two inch nails into boxes for ammunition. I said, "You can take it, but I want it back." She said, "I'll look after it, don't worry".

So Mum put it into her bag, and took it with her on the bus to work. All the women were fascinated when she produced it. She said, "Look what my daughter found". One of the men saw it, and I can't repeat his actual words here: something like, "Blimey Flo, you've got a bomb there and it's alive!" Mum called him a silly bugger and said, "My daughter has had it indoors for weeks and it's all right. You don't know what you're talking about. I'll put it under my bench." She had a box under her bench where she kept her bag, so she put it there and she's banging away at the bench hammering the nails in.

After work she took it home with her on the bus to show to her neighbours, and one of them swore it was alive and said she should take it to a warden. She brought it back to me and told me what he'd said, and I started getting a bit worried then, so I took it in to Joe, an air-raid warden who lived two doors from me. "What've you got there, Flo?", he said. "Well, I found this weeks ago. Is it all right?"

Well, he gave me such a talking to. "You've had it indoors how long? Do you realise that's alive? I'll have to take it away immediately, take it up the depot and get rid of it. I daren't tell them where I got it from. You'd be in serious trouble. I'll have to tell them a little white lie. I'll tell them I found it on one of the street shelter rooftops."

I was so upset, because I still didn't get my piece of shrapnel. The stupid things you do ...! My mum said, "To think, I carried it in my bag, and on the bus, carrying it to work. If only I'd known!"

FLO BATLEY

AGE EXCHANGE REMINISCENCE CENTRE

The Age Exchange Reminiscence Centre opened on 29th May 1987 at 11 Blackheath Village, London, S.E.3. This project has been established in response to a definite demand from the growing numbers interested in the field of reminiscence, either as trainers, as organisers of sessions, or as elderly participants in those sessions.

Pensioners are welcomed at the centre which is a magnet for those interested in talking and writing about their own lives. We offer them a drop-in centre where they can meet and discuss their current projects in a supportive and well equipped environment.

The Centre provides a resource and training centre for all those interested in developing skills in reminiscence work with elderly people in institutions. It also operates as a meeting place for those piloting new approaches to creative work with the elderly with reminiscence as a focus.

We stock the current literature on reminiscence and life history, mount exhibitions, and offer advice and support to care-workers and nursing staff across London who wish to try using these materials in their own settings.

Oral historians and those producing London life histories (their own and other people's) have access to our archives and are able to use our photographic and reprographic resources, as well as meeting others engaged in like activity for support and exchange of ideas.

Young people who are interested in volunteering work with the elderly, or those involved in oral history projects, are encouraged to come to the centre, to meet our members and look at our resources. We have also established a Youth Theatre which works on reminiscence shows with local pensioners, in what we feel to be a valuable bridge-building exercise.

We will always be needing reminiscence objects to stimulate recall. By this we mean unusual items which people may have stored in their attics, and no longer have a use for, but which would serve to remind older people about their earlier days. We are also grateful to anyone interested in helping in the centre during the day, on an occasional and voluntary basis.

If you are interested in knowing more about any of these activities please contact us on 081 318 9105/318 3504.